P9-AQL-958

Your Travel Guide to RENAISSANCE EUROPE

Your Travel Guide to
RENAISSANCE EUROPE

Nancy Day

RP RUNESTONE PRESS • MINNEAPOLIS

AN IMPRINT OF LERNER PUBLISHING GROUP

Designed by: Zachary Marell and Tim Parlin
Edited by: Katy Holmgren and Amy Boland
Illustrated by: Tim Parlin
Photo Researched by: Dan Mahoney

Runestone Press
An imprint of Lerner Publishing Group
241 First Avenue North
Minneapolis, Minnesota 55401 U.S.A.

Website address: www.lernerbooks.com

Library of Congress Cataloging-in-Publication Data

Day, Nancy.
    Your travel guide to Renaissance Europe / by Nancy Day.
      p.   cm.—(Passport to history)
    Includes bibliographical references and index.
    Summary: Takes readers on a journey back in time in order to experience life in Europe during the Renaissance, describing clothing, accommodations, foods, local customs, transportation, a few notable personalities, and more.
      ISBN: 0-8225-3080-5 (lib. bdg. : alk. paper)
      1. Europe Guidebooks—Juvenile literature. 2. Renaissance Guidebooks—Juvenile literature. [1. Renaissance. 2. Europe—Social life and customs.] I. Title. II. Series: Day, Nancy. Passport to history.

CB361.D35   2001   99-36805
914.04'599—dc21

Manufactured in the United States of America
2 3 4 5 6 7 – JR – 07 06 05 04 03 02

CONTENTS

INTRODUCTION

GETTING STARTED

Welcome to Passport to History. You will be traveling through time and space to Europe during a period called the Renaissance. This travel guide will answer questions such as:

➤ **What's up in Renaissance Europe?**

➤ **Where should I stay?**

➤ **What do I wear?**

➤ **Where can I find the best souvenirs?**

➤ **Who should I meet while I'm there?**

Remember, you are going back in time to a distant culture. Some of the things that you own didn't exist during the period you will visit, which didn't have electricity. That's why the pictures in this book are either drawings or photographs made after the invention of photography. So you can forget your video games, hair driers, cameras, medicines, watches, cell phones, and other modern conveniences that would make your stay a lot more comfortable. But don't worry. If you read this guide, you'll be able to do as the locals do—and they manage just fine, as you will see.

This map of Florence, Italy, dates to 1480.

NOTE TO THE TRAVELER

Modern-day people know a lot about what life was like during the Renaissance, which began in Italy in about A.D. 1350. The movement spread across Europe by 1400, and the period lasted until the 1580s. During this short period of history, the people of Renaissance Europe created documents, literature, artwork, and buildings that provide a window into their lives. Modern-day historians examine the structures and artifacts that survive. They get information from detailed paintings of religious and political events, medical drawings, sketches of inventions, and depictions of daily life.

7

The people of Renaissance Europe were eager to learn and to spread ideas. They left behind letters, diaries, histories, and stories of travels. Books such as *Lives of the Most Excellent Painters, Sculptors, and Architects,* written in 1550 by Giorgio Vasari, tells of the artistic achievements of the time. Modern readers can learn about the people Vasari describes and can figure out what he (and probably other people of the time) thought was important to know.

Artists, scientists, philosophers, historians, and religious scholars continue to study the Renaissance and evaluate its impact. Historians continue to improve their understanding of day-to-day life in Renaissance Europe. But even with all of this information, there are bound to be some differences between what modern-day experts think and the real thing. So although this book is a good starting point for your voyage to Renaissance Europe, please keep in mind that you might find that some things are a little different.

WHY VISIT RENAISSANCE EUROPE?

The Renaissance was one of the most exciting periods of human history. People looked back into history and came up with new ways to look at the world. People studied the ideas of the ancient Greeks and Romans, who had ruled vast empires in ancient times. The Greek Empire had dominated parts of the Mediterranean region (the area surrounding the Mediterranean Sea) from 490 B.C. to 146 B.C. The Roman Empire, based in Rome, Italy, came after the Greek Empire. During both periods, scholars, politicians, writers, and mathematicians investigated the world around them and wrote down their thoughts, beliefs, and observations.

TAKE IT *from a Local*

[It is] as if on a given signal, splendid talents are stirring.

—*scholar Desiderius Erasmus, 1517*

RENAISSANCE EUROPE, 1500s

ENGLAND
London

NETHERLANDS

RHINELAND

HOLY ROMAN
EMPIRE

Paris

FRENCH
STATES

ATLANTIC
OCEAN

Venice

VENICE

MILAN

Florence

NAVARRE

Lisbon

ARAGON

FLORENCE

Rome

PAPAL
STATES

NAPLES
Naples

PORTUGAL

CASTILE

MEDITERRANEAN SEA

Messina

GRANADA

AFRICA

N

0   100   200   300
in miles

0   100   200   300
in kilometers

At its height, the Roman Empire controlled northernmost Africa, most of Europe, and parts of the Middle East. Trade between different parts of the empire flourished. But the empire crumbled under the force of invasions and political problems. Around the year 500, the Roman Empire began to dissolve. The period known as the Middle Ages, or the Medieval period, began.

Universities were founded and flourished during this time. But on the whole, very few medieval people could read or write. Art and science were no longer a part of everyday life. Most Christian Europeans forgot classical (ancient Greek and Roman) ideas. Classical thinking stayed alive only in the Byzantine Empire of eastern and southeastern Europe and in the Islamic Empire of the Middle East and North Africa.

The Middle Ages were a time of danger, war, and disease. Droughts and other natural disasters swept through Europe. Famines (periods of starvation) often followed. Wars and invasions kept people heavily guarded and always on the lookout. Travel became more dangerous, so fewer trade routes flourished. And plagues (rapidly spreading diseases) killed more than one-third of all Europeans in the 1300s.

The Renaissance began slowly in Italy. This region wasn't involved in as many wars as other parts of Europe. Italian cities became rich from trade on the Mediterranean Sea. Some rich folks decided to encourage and support artists and thinkers. Italian poets began to read the works of ancient Roman scholars. They thought about how the old ideas made sense in their own lives.

Renaissance scholars are interested in a range of topics, including art, religion, government, and science.

Renaissance inventors improve firing mechanisms for guns. They build multiple looms for manufacturing cloth. Inventors create water-powered machines that crush stone to make it easier to extract (take out) minerals. Curiosity and creativity lead to these and other practical solutions to problems in science, business, war, and daily life.

By 1350 the Renaissance began to sweep across Europe. Life changed for many people. Scholars, scientists, artists, writers, and philosophers studied classical works of art and writings to see what they could learn. People again became interested in poetry, law, history, and philosophy. Music and art blossomed. A group of scholars called humanists explored language, social studies, and philosophy. Others tackled anatomy, mathematics, and physics. People created new ideas of the world and their place in it. People also began to question religion and the leaders of their churches.

New inventions changed how people lived. The printing press, invented in the 1400s, made books cheaper, which helped spread ideas and made it possible for many people to buy books. To the people living in the 1400s, it seemed as if the world had awakened from a thousand-year sleep. They called the Middle Ages the "Dark Ages." They named their own era the Renaissance, a French word meaning "rebirth."

THE BASICS

Castles and towns dot the European countryside during the Renaissance.

LOCATION LOWDOWN

Forget modern-day Europe when you visit during the Renaissance. England, Scotland, and Ireland aren't Great Britain yet. What we think of as France and Spain are actually made up of smaller countries. Borders shift and change with wars and as kings and queens marry, joining their territories. King Ferdinand of Sicily and Naples (both part of Italy in modern times) also rules Castile (part of Spain). His marriage to Queen Isabella of Aragon brings together parts of Spain, and they conquer most of the rest of the region. The Holy Roman Empire once included nearly all of Europe. In the 1400s, it becomes known as the Holy Roman Empire of the German Nation—Germany, for short. It's a huge kingdom with twenty million people. The Papal States—lands controlled by the Roman Catholic pope—are sprinkled across Italy and other parts of Europe. Small areas called city-states make up most of Italy. The Italian city-states of Naples, Venice, Milan, Florence, and the Papal States have their own laws and ways of life. The Italian city-states control large areas and fight each other for territory, wealth, and power. The Netherlands, the Rhineland (part of the Holy Roman Empire), and northern Italy are Europe's most urban areas.

Fewer than seventy-three million people live in Renaissance Europe. All of England has fewer people than the modern metropolitan area (city and suburbs) of Chicago. The largest cities are Paris, Naples, and Venice. Each has a population of about 150,000 people. But Europe is in the middle of a population explosion. From 1500 to 1600, many cities double their populations. Lisbon, Portugal, and Messina, Italy, triple in size. London quadruples. Crime increases as the populations swell.

But don't be surprised if you have trouble even finding a town or city. You can walk for days through the thick forests that spread over much of Europe without coming across a village. Over 80 percent of the locals live in tiny villages, and even these are at least fifteen or twenty miles apart. (That's about a day's walk.) And keep in mind that the countryside is dangerous. Wild animals such as bears, boars, bison, lynx, and wolves roam the forests.

LOCAL TIME

If you visit in October 1582, prepare for some confusion. Up until this time, folks have used the Julian calendar, which Julius Caesar, a Roman emperor, set up in 46 B.C. Caesar declared that April, June, September, and November would each have thirty days, February would have twenty-eight days, and all the other months would have thirty-one days. He also ordered leap years (every four years, February has twenty-nine days). Sounds familiar, right? This system (the Julian calendar)

Peasants harvest a field of grain. For many Renaissance country people, life revolves around farming.

was supposed to match the length of the solar year, or the time that it takes the earth to complete its orbit around the sun.

But the Julian calendar is actually about eleven minutes too long. Year by year, this extra time has added up, and in 1582 the calendar is off by ten whole days. To set things right, Pope Gregory XIII sets up a new Gregorian (get it?) calendar. He decrees that in 1582, the day after October fourth will be October fifteenth. He then rules that years ending in "00" will become leap years only if they are divisible by four hundred. This corrects the calendar so that it is closer to the actual solar year. Non-Roman Catholic countries are slow to accept this new Gregorian calendar, and people grumble about "losing" ten days.

CLIMATE

The climate varies across Renaissance Europe. In most regions, the weather is mild. Temperatures seldom fall far below freezing in winter. And it doesn't get much hotter than about eighty degrees in the summer. Weather is warmer along the Mediterranean Sea. In winter in northern Europe, frozen rivers may delay boat travel.

Winter weather can be a problem in the Alps, a mountain range in central Europe. You can run into significant snows in the winter. Watch your step! The icy slopes get slippery and dangerous. Springtime clouds can make the Alps pretty gloomy, too.

LANGUAGE LESSON

Europeans speak many different languages. Common folk speak their local language, such as Spanish, English, French, German, and Tuscan (Italian). Scientists, officials, judges, and priests speak Latin, which was the language of ancient Rome (although it has changed some since then). Some people would like to see Latin become the universal language of Europe.

The languages you'll hear in Renaissance Europe sound pretty different than in modern times. Even in England you may have some trouble catching on. People don't have the same accent as they do in modern times, and the vocabulary is different. (Think of the way people speak in Shakespeare's plays.) You'll find that people speak in many different dialects, or versions, of each language. Charles de Rouelles travels across France in the 1500s. He reports that he hears eight different ways of saying "yes" and "no."

THE NAME GAME

During the Renaissance, people begin to use last names. You will meet people who have taken their last name from their job, such as Miller (someone who mills grain), Taylor (tailor), or Smith (blacksmith). Some people take the name of a local lord or noble. A person could be known as "John's son," creating the last name "Johnson."

Another local custom is to add a descriptive term to a name, such as "Jacob the Rich." Note that a person may spell his or her name in various ways. Krupp, Krup, Krupe, and even Krapp may be the same person. The locals don't think there is one right way to spell a word.

For the most part, Renaissance Europeans name their kids whatever they like. In Geneva, Switzerland, however, the law states that every baby has to be named after a figure in the Bible.

WHICH CITIES TO VISIT

CITY LIFE

You'll want to spend most of your visit in the bustling, exciting cities of the Renaissance—especially Rome, Venice, and Florence. In these city-states, you'll find the era in full flower. Thick, sturdy walls—often with towers—protect cities and townspeople from invaders. Armed guards stand at gates that are shut at certain times during the day and at night. When you pass through a city gate, the guards will examine your travel papers. They'll check to make sure that you haven't been in a plague-infested area in the last forty days. It'll help if you have a letter naming a local citizen who will watch out for you. Small bribes won't hurt, either.

In this painting of an ideal city, people bustle in the streets and shop owners run brisk businesses.

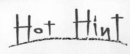

Hot Hint

If you leave the city during the day, be sure to return before the guards shut the gates at sundown. They won't reopen the gates for anyone until morning.

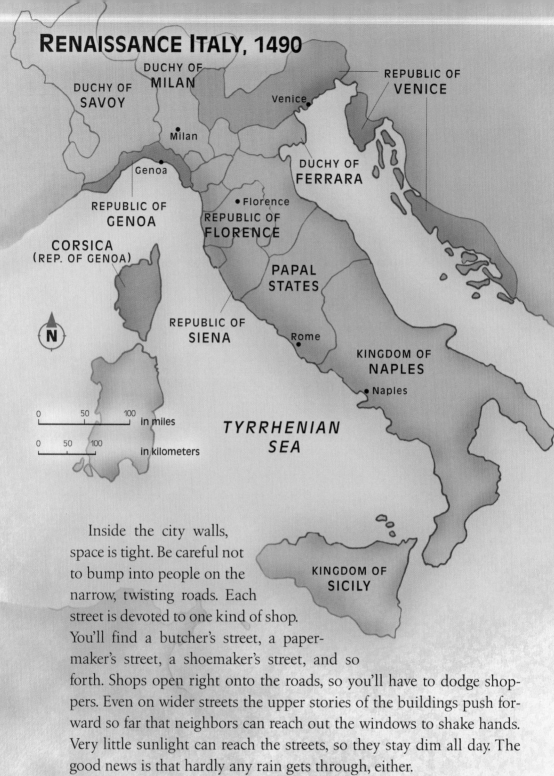

RENAISSANCE ITALY, 1490

DUCHY OF SAVOY

DUCHY OF MILAN

REPUBLIC OF VENICE

Venice

Milan

Genoa

DUCHY OF FERRARA

REPUBLIC OF GENOA

CORSICA
(REP. OF GENOA)

Florence

REPUBLIC OF FLORENCE

PAPAL STATES

N

REPUBLIC OF SIENA

Rome

KINGDOM OF NAPLES

Naples

0   50   100
in miles

0   50   100
in kilometers

TYRRHENIAN SEA

KINGDOM OF SICILY

Inside the city walls, space is tight. Be careful not to bump into people on the narrow, twisting roads. Each street is devoted to one kind of shop. You'll find a butcher's street, a paper-maker's street, a shoemaker's street, and so forth. Shops open right onto the roads, so you'll have to dodge shoppers. Even on wider streets the upper stories of the buildings push forward so far that neighbors can reach out the windows to shake hands. Very little sunlight can reach the streets, so they stay dim all day. The good news is that hardly any rain gets through, either.

It's easy to lose your way. You'll spot few, if any, street signs (reading is just becoming common). Many travelers make a point to climb to the top of a tall building or tower to get the lay of the land. You'll recognize churches by their spires or domes. Be sure to look for a building with a large square tower. This is the donjon—the secular, or non-religious, center for the city. The donjon serves as a shelter in the event of a catastrophe. This is also where the town council meets to vote on city issues. Watchmen stand on the roof of the donjon twenty-four hours a day. If they spot an attack or a fire, they ring a bell to warn the city's people. The donjon's basement houses the dungeon . . . and the executioner.

FLORENCE

Florence, located in northern Italy, is at the center of the Renaissance. This wealthy city is home to about seventy thousand people, including many of the finest artists, scientists, and writers. The city and its wealthy families provide money for beautiful cathedrals and for stunning works of art.

Visit the wonderful palace in the Piazza Santa Trinita. Locals tell a story about this palace. Three brothers learn that one of their ships has docked in nearby Pisa with valuable cargo. To sell it, someone has to set

This painting shows part of Florence's famed Piazza Santa Trinita.

the prices. The two older brothers don't want to miss their afternoon nap. While they sleep, the younger brother, Bartolini Salimbene, gallops to Pisa and sells the cargo for a fortune. He uses the money to build the Piazza Santa Trinita. If you look above the windows, you will see Bartolini's motto: *Per non dormire*. Roughly translated, the phrase means, "you snooze, you lose."

If you need a place to stay, you will find that Florentine inns are all on the same street. Strict regulations assure that you'll be treated well at any of them.

ROME

Don't visit Rome in the early years of the Renaissance. In the 1300s, Rome has only about twenty thousand inhabitants. The city's buildings are decaying. Rubble fills the streets. Sheep and goats graze on the hillsides.

But that changes in the 1400s. Rome is the seat of the Roman Catholic Church, the religion of most of Renaissance Europe. Pope Nicholas V has a vision for a new Rome that will rival the city of classical times, when it was the heart of the Roman Empire. Pope Nicholas V begins rebuilding projects. The popes who follow him continue the

Boaters travel up and down the Tiber River, which runs through Rome.

efforts. They hire famous architects such as Michelangelo and Raphael to make the city beautiful again. Through their efforts, the Vatican (an area of Rome) becomes the site of some of the Renaissance's greatest artistic achievements. Rome becomes a must-see for every visitor.

You'll find many other travelers if you visit Rome, but they aren't tourists. Most European pilgrims (travelers to religious sites) head to Rome. You will be able to buy maps and religious guidebooks that show the locations of important religious sites in Rome. You may want to visit Rome's seven great churches. Each offers a special blessing to visiting pilgrims. Rome is also home to many objects with religious importance. For example, St. Peter's Church contains what people believe to be the spear that, according to the Bible, was used to stab Jesus at the cross.

In 1527 Rome is sacked (captured and destroyed) by German and Spanish mercenaries (soldiers for hire). Thousands die and the Pope is jailed by the conquerors. We suggest you avoid this terrible event. It marks the beginning of the end of the Renaissance.

VENICE

Venice, with a population of about 150,000, rests on Italy's northeastern coast. Venice controls a large area in Italy, part of the eastern coast of the Adriatic Sea, and the Mediterranean islands of Crete and Cyprus. Traders bring luxury goods from Scandinavia, other parts of Europe, India, and the Middle East to Venice. Venice is built on a series of tiny islands in the lagoon formed by the mouths of the Po and Piave Rivers. People get around the city on gondolas, flat-bottomed boats propelled by a single oar.

If you visit Venice, be sure to look for an official guide who will show you where to stay, what to see, and where to shop. Ask to check out the "mouths of truth." These masks are carved into the stone walls of government buildings. They're like a crime hotline. Inside the open mouths are slots where you can secretly insert a slip of paper. On the paper, people write their name and the name of a person they know has committed a crime. If the authorities find that the accusation is false, the accuser gets fined. Otherwise, the criminal is punished.

MONEY MATTERS

A banker and his wife count money and check their records of the day's business.

A DUCAT FOR YOUR THOUGHTS

Europeans in the Renaissance use many kinds of coins. You may run across pfennigs, hellers, écus, florins, gulden, orrt, anglots, ducats, and stuivers. These coins are made from gold or silver. Printed on each coin is a value that should equal how much metal is in the coin. Sometimes people shave off a little metal from a coin and keep the shavings. This reduces the coin's value, so you'll want to weigh each coin to see how much it's really worth. By the way, paper money doesn't exist here. Locals drag coins around in baglike purses, which get pretty heavy.

Some people don't bother with money. They trade valuable items, such as spices, for other goods. If you hear someone talking about "black gold," don't get too excited. It's just pepper. But black pepper is easy to sell for a profit, which is nothing to sneeze at. In the 1530s, the king of Portugal orders lavish tapestries (weavings). He pays the bill in pepper. You may want to fill your pockets with peppercorns before you go to Renaissance Europe.

During the 1500s, about 240,000 Europeans sail to the Americas. Most are Spaniards who are seeking their fortunes. The fare is equivalent to nearly two month's salary for a skilled artisan.

Pepper and other spices are valuable because traders have to travel great distances over land and sea to reach far-off spots like India, Sri Lanka, and the Spice Islands (in modern-day Indonesia), where the spices grow. The voyage is slow and dangerous in the small ships of the Renaissance. In 1498 Portuguese explorer and trader Vasco da Gama successfully sails all around Africa to reach the Spice Islands, but this doesn't bring down the value of spices.

WHERE TO FIND MONEY

You'll need different money in almost every city you visit, especially in Italy. It might be a good idea to deposit your money in a bank and get a letter of credit instead. A letter of credit works sort of like a modern-day traveler's check. Cash the letter at a bank to receive an equal amount in the other country's or city's currency (type of money).

Nearly every town has a money changer who will trade your money for the local currency. If you don't have money to exchange, you can pledge an object (a jacket, for example) at a *presto*, or pawnbroker. There are several prestos in Florence. To get your item back, you'll have to pay more than the amount you received, so this shouldn't be your first choice.

If you're desperate, you can try borrowing some cash from wealthy merchants. These merchants have so much money that they can afford to lend some. The borrowers pay fees, called interest, for the privilege.

Careful records, letters of credit, and cash are the banker's stock in trade during the Renaissance.

Even emperors and kings borrow money from rich merchant bankers. The rulers borrow to pay for personal luxuries, for political operations, and for wars. This makes the bankers (who can be found in every city) important and powerful.

The top moneylending merchant is Jakob Fugger, also known as "Jakob the Rich." From his home in Augsburg, Germany, Jakob the Rich becomes one of the most powerful men in Europe. By 1491 Fugger is so rich that he lends money to the duke of Tyrol (part of the Holy Roman Empire).

In exchange, Fugger gets the rights to Tyrolean copper and silver mines. (During the Renaissance, rulers own all mines and their contents.) When the duke becomes the Holy Roman Emperor Maximilian I in 1493, he borrows even more money from Fugger. The banker gets mines in Hungary. In this way, Fugger basically comes to control Europe's supply of silver.

Prices

OF COMMON GOODS

Small, unbound book—1 ducat

Horse—6 ducats

Gold helmet covered with 174 gems, including rubies, diamonds, pearls, and emeralds (carrying case included)—144,400 ducats

Yearly salary for a servant—7 ducats

Yearly salary for a senior administrator—90 ducats

Yearly salary for a lecturer or professor—100 to 150 ducats

HOW TO
GET AROUND

Travel by cart is common in Renaissance Europe.

During the Renaissance, few people go farther than fifteen miles from home. Some don't leave their city at all. Men may travel to find work, to go to school, or to practice a trade. Women travel from their homes to visit family, shop at a market, or to attend church. Long-distance travelers are usually pilgrims or merchants. Pilgrims travel to Rome, to the Holy Land, or to Santiago de Compostela, a religious site in Spain.

Because the wilderness between cities isn't very safe, many people travel in groups. To go a long distance, be prepared to go from cart to boat to horse to raft to foot and back again to reach your destination. Renaissance Europe doesn't have superhighways, trains, or airplanes that go directly to a destination.

By Land

If you visit in the early years of the Renaissance, you'll notice that the roads are terrible. The thousand-year-old stone roads built by the ancient Romans are the best ones around. But don't be too surprised if parts of them seem to be missing. Over the years, builders have taken many of the stones to make churches, houses, and barns. Most roads are no more than dirt paths that turn into mud after a rainstorm. The road might seem to vanish into the muddy fields. And if people need some dirt or clay, they usually just dig it out of the street. They leave behind deep pits.

When you're traveling overland, remember the rules of the road. By local custom, an empty cart must yield (pull over to the side) for a full cart. A horse and rider must give way to a cart, a walker must allow a horse and rider to pass, and all travelers must stop to let pass someone who is being chased on foot or on horseback.

Most locals simply walk to get where they need to go. Carrying your pack, you can travel fifteen miles a day. That's remembering that you'll run into bad weather, slow-to-climb hills, and rivers. You'll need to pack a bag with something to eat—bread and cheese works well. A heavy

cloak that can double as a blanket is a must. Don't forget money, flints to spark fires, and something to drink. You may wish to copy pilgrims, who carry a staff (a long walking stick). It might seem clumsy to carry at first, but the staff comes in handy on the road. Use it for testing the depth of streams, for leaning on while climbing uphill, and for waving at hungry stray dogs. A good stick is especially useful for whacking would-be robbers.

The fastest way to travel overland is on horseback. Riders can travel eighteen to thirty miles a day. But even if you're used to horseback riding, you may be in for an unpleasant surprise. Renaissance saddles have little padding and no horn to grab for balance. As a German merchant observed in the 1500s, "I have had so little respite that my bottom has been constantly a-fire from the saddle." And keep in mind that horses cost a lot—more than a car costs in modern times.

A horseman rides home to his castle.

Sea captain Ferdinand Magellan began the world's first known voyage around the globe in his ship Victoria, *which was accompanied by four other vessels.*

You may be able to pay for a ride in a cart pulled by oxen, mules, or horses. Most carts haul goods but may also pick up a few passengers. Carts are covered, so you'll stay dry if it rains. The carts bump and bounce painfully over the rough roads. After about 1470, carriages come into use. Because a carriage's front section moves independently to make steering easier, the ride is a little smoother. In the 1500s, you'll spot enclosed coaches, with a high, outside seat for the driver. Kings,

TAKE IT from a Local

There is no sea unnavigable, no land uninhabitable.

—*merchant Robert Thorne, five years after Magellan's expedition to sail around the globe returned to Europe in 1522*

SIDE TRIP TRIVIA

In the 1400s, wealthy Europeans loved to season their food with expensive spices from the Indies, which they knew was somewhere to the east. To get spices, people relied on foreign merchants who kept their routes secret. Many European rulers, including King Ferdinand and Queen Isabella of Spain, were eager to find the way to India so they could cash in on the rich spice trade. A Genoese sea captain named Cristoforo Colombo came to Ferdinand and Isabella with the theory that a boat could reach the Indies by going west across the Atlantic Ocean. In 1492 they decided to put some money on his wild idea and set up an expedition for him. Well, he didn't find India, but he certainly did find something....

queens, and other wealthy people favor these grand vehicles. Keep in mind that weather is a much bigger concern here than it is at home. Enclosed coaches have windows but no glass for protection. Passengers in all vehicles deal with mosquitoes, mud, wind, rain, and snow.

Few of Renaissance Europe's many rivers and streams are crossed by bridges. The bridges that do exist may be rickety, so look for a ford (a shallow area to cross). If there is no ford, you may find a ferryboat, but this service can be expensive.

BY WATER

The locals use the rivers like roads. Traveling downstream with the current, a boat can float between sixty and ninety miles in a single day. For example, it takes about twenty-four hours to get from Lyons, France, to Avignon, France, by floating down the Rhône River. But the return trip upstream (against the current) takes a month. Horses or oxen walking along the shore pull the boat upstream on ropes.

Within some cities, canals serve as streets and people get around on small boats. Most boats carry goods and passengers. But some boats are the goods. You may travel by wooden raft on the Rhine River in Germany. At the end of the trip, workers send the raft to sawmills.

To travel along the Atlantic, Mediterranean, and Baltic coasts, you can sail by ship. But beware! The crowded ships are uncomfortable. Follow the advice of one local—make friends with the ship's captain to get a sleeping space on deck. It's a better place to sleep than underneath the deck, where the heat and the smell of people can be fierce.

Now for the bad news: the bathroom is in the very front of the ship. Cold waves splash up into the bathroom area. For this reason, many passengers waiting in line simply take off their clothes to keep them dry.

DUTIES & MAPS

If you travel through more than one country, you may pass through checkpoints. Some savvy travelers carry passports. If you get one, the document will describe you, the others you're traveling with, the number of horses with you, and the amount of money you are carrying. If it is a time of war (and it often is), your passport may forbid you to enter enemy countries.

Don't be nervous at the checkpoints! The guards are there mostly to collect a duty (tax). How much you pay will depend on how much luggage you have. That's because the duties are in place to tax merchants carrying lots of goods from country to country. If you travel by water between Frankfurt and Cologne (in Germany), you will pay at least ten tolls (fees for using a road, bridge, shipping lane, or other route). When you pass through a city, cross a body of water, or travel over private lands, you will be expected to pay up, too.

If you get lost, a map won't help very much. In the early years of the Renaissance, you'll be surprised to see that the maps show three continents—Asia, Africa, and Europe—of roughly equal size. And sometimes the continents are mislabeled. All three continents are inside a circle, with Jerusalem at the center. In the early Renaissance, many people believe that Jerusalem is God's chosen center of the world.

Later in the Renaissance, people use math to better understand geography, distance, and measurements. Map making becomes a popular hobby. People make maps of roads, canals, forts, and lavish homes. Some maps show which ruler controls what area (this changes often during the Renaissance). Other maps don't even show the borders between countries—much less the roads you'll be walking. Some of the hand-drawn maps are beautiful. You might want to get one as a souvenir.

LOCAL CUSTOMS & MANNERS

Music, dancing, and feasting mark village celebrations.

WHAT YOU CAN EXPECT FROM THE LOCALS

Within Europe, many locals may make nasty remarks about each other. You may hear people say that the English are proud, the French are violent, or the Italians are cowards. These comments get quite ugly in times of war. During the Swabian War of 1499, Germans insult their Swiss enemies by calling them "cow-herds" and "milkers." The French call the English "hideous, loathsome, stinking, and reeking tailed toads."

Politics

Feudalism was common in the Middle Ages. In feudalism, a lord runs a huge estate (land). Serfs (peasants) work the land, and the lord provides military protection. The system still exists during the Renaissance, but you'll find somewhat different political systems in the countries you visit. Spain, England, France, Poland, Denmark, and Portugal have monarchies (rule by a king or queen). In England a king (or queen) rules with the help of a small council. The members of England's House of Lords inherit their positions. But the House of Lords meets only when royalty thinks it would be a good idea. That isn't very often. England's House of Commons has elected representatives. In central Italy, where the Papal States are, the Pope rules. Seven powerful men elect the Holy Roman Emperor. France's Anjou family rules the Kingdom of Naples in southern Italy. Councils govern some city-states in Italy. In Venice, Florence, and Genoa, a group of people—all men— can vote to elect council members.

Charles d'Amboise, a member of a noble French family, is governor of Milan in 1500.

THE SOCIAL SCENE

Renaissance society has different social levels. The very sick and very poor people are the "lowest" level. These people rely on charity, churches, and hospitals. Above the poor are the peasants, who make up 80 to 90 percent of the local population. A peasant may work for someone else as a laborer in a city. In the countryside, peasants rent farm fields from rich landowners. Some peasants work as servants for rich families.

In towns and cities, the middle class is the next level. In Italy this group is known as the *popolo minuto,* the "little people." Shopkeepers, craftspeople, butchers, bakers, artists, schoolteachers, carpenters, lawyers, and government workers make up the middle class. Most belong to guilds—large groups representing particular professions. Each skilled craft—lace making, stone carving, glove making, and so on—has its own guild. Some guilds are wealthy and powerful. These include the guilds of cloth merchants, wool manufacturers, and bankers.

IMPORTANT
Safety Tip

Being disrespectful to one's "betters" is taken seriously here. One child who hit his parents has his head cut off.

The wealthiest citizens, known in Italy as the *ricchi* (the rich), are born into old, noble families. Most nobles inherit money, land, and political power. Noblemen are the real movers and shakers in Renaissance Europe. They serve as patrons (sponsors) of famous artists, scientists, and explorers. They also control the political system, and some lead armies.

Most noble ladies have few rights. But some noblewomen achieve equality with men. Isabella d'Este rules Mantua (a city-state in Italy) after her husband, the Marquis of Mantua, is captured in a war with Venice. At the end of the Renaissance, Queen Elizabeth I succeeds Queen Mary to the throne of England. Queen Elizabeth I holds the throne from 1558 to 1603. Under her rule, England's navy comes to dominate the seas of Europe. In modern times, the years of her rule are remembered as the Elizabethan Age.

SLAVERY

Slavery isn't common in Renaissance Europe, but it is present. Most slaves are prisoners of war, criminals, or captives taken in raids. They are traded as if they were salt, spices, or horses. Some come from Africa. Others come from Russia, Romania, or other places.

DAY-TO-DAY LIFE

During the Renaissance, people wake up early and go to bed early. Without electrical lights, people work when the sun is shining. On a farm, women and men work side by side. Men plough and mow fields, while women tie sheaves (bundles of grain) and turn hay to keep it from rotting in piles. Children help out in the fields. They work every day except for Sunday, which is a day of rest.

In towns and cities, many young people begin training to be members of a guild. Preteen and teenage boys are apprenticed to (work under) a master, who is very skilled at a craft. After seven to ten years

People have to get up with the sun to spend a day in the fields.

36

An artist's apprentice prepares ingredients for paint.

of learning a trade and working without pay, an apprentice becomes a journeyman. That means he can work for whomever he chooses. Usually a master hires him as a skilled helper. After perfecting his skills, a journeyman can pay a large fee to take a test to become a master himself. The fee goes to the guild, which judges his work on—you guessed it—his masterpiece. Some workers remain journeymen their entire lives. They may lack the skills of a master. Guilds may make it hard for journeymen to even take the test. The guilds might only let the sons of masters take the test, or they might set their fees so high that few of the low-paid journeymen can pay.

Masters and other middle-class men spend their days at work in their businesses. They teach their apprentices and do the most difficult or delicate work. Women manage their family's daily lives. They do the household work (or supervise servants who do). For example, they're in charge of buying, storing, and cooking food.

Most guilds do not allow women. But some guilds, such as lace making and laundering, are for women only. Wives of masters are active in the family business. The women might keep track of the family's money. Some guilds even have rules that wives must sell the goods. A widow might keep her husband's business going until her son is old enough to take it over. And this is on top of managing the household.

Few Renaissance women actually run major businesses. In the 1560s, however, Susanne Erker is "manager-mistress" of an important mint (a place where money is made) in Bohemia (in modern times, part of the Czech Republic). A few women run ferries or work in shops. Women might volunteer for charitable organizations, such as hospitals that serve the poor or sick.

LOCAL MANNERS

As far as table manners go, locals are pretty casual. Napkins haven't been invented yet. You may be warned against wiping your mouth on the tablecloth, but feel free to use your sleeve. And you can gnaw on huge bones at the table.

Even the best-dressed locals wipe their noses on their sleeves. You will be relieved to learn that nobles, kings, and queens do not follow this disgusting practice. No—they wipe their noses on their servant's sleeves!

It's not rude to feed your crumbs to the dogs in Renaissance Europe.

If you are unsure how to behave, look for a book on manners. The guides advise against hawking up phlegm, belching, and passing gas. Erasmus, a famous Dutch humanist, writes *De Civilitate,* a book offering social advice to young people. Humanists believe that courtesy is a way of showing respect. So Erasmus mentions that sneezing in other people's faces is rude. If your clothes smell, he suggests changing them. And he says not to spit food on the table. Instead, put the unwanted bits in your hand and toss them on the floor for the dogs to eat.

Now Hear This

When you have blown your nose, you should not open your handkerchief and inspect it, as though pearls or rubies had dropped out of your skull.
—*Giovanni della Casa,* Il Galateo, *a book on polite behavior in 1558*

LOCAL BELIEFS

Most Europeans during the Renaissance are Roman Catholics. (Russian Orthodox and Greek Orthodox Christians live at the eastern edges of Europe.) In large towns, between one and three out of every hundred people are priests, nuns, or other clerics (religious workers). The local church is an important place in every town. Most people attend Mass (religious service) almost every day. Some wealthy families build churches or donate elaborate artworks.

In some parts of Renaissance Europe, Christians, Muslims, and Jews live and work in the same areas. This is true in Spain, but only if you visit before 1492. In that year, King Ferdinand and Queen Isabella conquer the Muslim-controlled province of Granada. The victory unites Spain as a Christian state. Then the king and queen declare that everyone has to follow government rules about clothing, ways of life, and religion. They command Jews and Muslims to convert to Christianity or to leave Spain. If they don't obey, they'll be killed—and many are. Some convert (or pretend to). Others escape to North Africa, parts of southern France, and, in the sixteenth century, the Americas.

In 1478 Catholic Church officials and Spain's government create the Spanish Inquisition—a group of judges who investigate heretics (people who don't follow Church teachings). The Spanish Inquisition executes thousands of accused heretics, who are considered enemies of the state.

In the later years of the Renaissance, new religions are born. In about 1520, a Catholic priest named Martin Luther protests practices of the Catholic Church. After a long struggle, the Church excommunicates (kicks out) Luther. He becomes a major founder of Protestantism, a group of new, non-Catholic religions. In Geneva, a reformer named John Calvin founds Presbyterianism. In 1534 King Henry VIII of England creates the Church of England. By the 1550s, Catholics and Protestants all across Europe are fighting for control of governments, for military power, and for the loyalty of ordinary people. Wars break out and people are jailed or even killed for their beliefs. Intolerance on both sides makes life dangerous.

You'll find the locals also believe in black magic and witchcraft. If a woman dies, you may see the family emptying all household containers of water so that her soul doesn't drown. If a cat or dog runs across the coffin, some folks believe the dead person will turn into a vampire.

You will also hear people discussing astrology. Locals believe that the earth is fixed in place at the center of rotating spheres containing the moon, the planets, the sun, and other stars. They think that the movements of the spheres influence their lives. Astrologers calculate these movements and use them to predict the future and to understand the present and the past. People consult astrologers for advice.

Hot Hint

Locals with gray hair and stooped bodies may only be in their thirties. Very few Renaissance people reach their fifties or even their forties. Someone in her thirties might be known as "Old Hannah." (Don't try this one at home.)

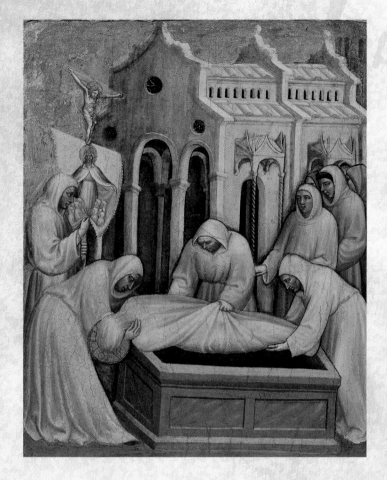

Mourners lay a dead person in a stone tomb. The body is wrapped in a white sheet called a burial shroud.

DEATH & BEYOND

Renaissance Europeans believe in an afterlife (life after death). Wealthy merchants plan for the afterlife with great care. They set aside money for religious groups and for charity to make sure their souls will end up in heaven. Believers may leave money to priests or nuns to pray for their souls.

In Florence people follow strict rules for funerals. Undertakers dress the body simply and place a plain cap on its head. They remove women's rings, unless they're of little value. The mourners wear black mourning clothes. (Wearers reuse the black fabric to make everyday clothes later.) The burial is usually inside a church or special burial building. Only two small candles or torches light the ceremony. The locals figure that the dead don't need the light, so anything more is a waste. Fancy funeral dinners aren't allowed, either. Only two courses can be served.

WHAT TO WEAR

CLOTHES

Clothes show more than your sense of style here. In fact, clothes are almost like a uniform. For example, only nobles wear fur. In some areas, you can be arrested for wearing fur if you are not of noble birth. Heretics wear crosses sewn on their shirts. Jews, by law, must wear a large yellow circle on their shirts. Don't wear a gray coat and a red hat. That is the costume of a leper, someone who has Hansen's disease.

Certain types of fabrics and dyes can show someone's wealth. One strong shade of red comes from a dye made by grinding up cochineal beetles. This pricey, imported dye colors the turbans that rich merchants wear.

Rich folks may have big wardrobes. Lucrezia Borgia, the Duchess of Ferrara and member of a powerful Italian family, boasts fifty gowns, twenty hats, thirty-three pairs of shoes, and sixty pairs of slippers. But peasants might not even have a change of clothes.

The locals look for ways to stand out, whether it's scented gloves, pink capes, velvet shoes, or thick gold

Now Hear This

Anyone whose legs are too thin, or exceptionally fat, or perhaps crooked, should not wear vivid or parti-colored hose, in order not to attract attention to his defects.
— *Giovanni della Casa*, Il Galateo

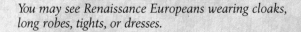

You may see Renaissance Europeans wearing cloaks, long robes, tights, or dresses.

This fair-skinned, blond young woman represents the Renaissance European ideal of female beauty. The painter has pictured her holding a unicorn to show her purity.

chains—and that's just the men! Men can pick brightly colored hose (tights), pointed hats, and velvet coats. Women choose dresses made from beautifully patterned fabrics. Some gowns are stitched with pearls or gold thread.

Religious pilgrims wear long robes gathered at the waist. Pilgrims also wear capes, called pelerines, which double as blankets at night. Wide-brimmed hats keep off the rain and shield their faces from the sun. You may also know them by their staffs.

For traveling, men will need a large hat, boots, breeches (pants that end just under the knee), and gloves. Women wear dresses at all times. Simple ones are recommended for traveling. Females will also put on hats or caps, capes, and gloves.

HAIR

Long, blond hair is very fashionable for women. Some women use bleaches to get the look. Others sit in the sun to lighten their hair. Females who feel that they don't have enough hair can buy a bundle of fake hair made of silk or of someone else's real hair. Bundles of blond curls are especially popular, even though many women cover their hair with caps most of the time. Men's hairstyles are getting shorter than women's, and some men wear pointy beards.

BEAUTY

You may notice that the local adults seem small. An average man here is only a little over five feet tall and weighs about 135 pounds. Women are even smaller. You'll definitely notice that the locals aren't too keen on bathing or washing their hair. Renaissance Europeans prefer lots of perfume to baths. Scented gloves are popular, for example. But combined with the perfume people splash all over and their personal odors—the effect can be a little, well, powerful. The Europeans may wash their clothes only a few times a year.

Cosmetics and beauty treatments are not as common in the Renaissance as in modern days. Women use tweezers to pluck unwanted hair. Be careful about trying makeup—some contain poisons that cause sicknesses or that eat away at skin. Many women blend their own makeup using secret recipes. For example, some women boil a dove and then apply the liquid to their bodies for beautiful skin.

Women prize a white complexion. Out in the sun, women wear broad-brimmed hats to keep from tanning. Women in Venice often wear veils when walking in the streets.

Aristocrats wear plenty of jewelry. Women put on earrings, necklaces, bracelets, and rings. No knight would be caught dead without his signet ring (a ring carved with his initials or a special pattern). You may also see men wearing decorative daggers or swords and even gold medals.

Hot Hint

Religious pilgrims bathe in certain streams that they believe have healing powers. Follow their lead and at least you'll stay clean!

What to
See & Do

Sites to See

The Vatican The Vatican, in Rome, is the seat (headquarters) of the Pope. The Vatican slowly becomes famous for its huge library and its magnificent works of art. Don't miss the fresco (wall painting) by the famous artist Raphael. Titled *The School of Athens,* it appears in the Vatican Stanze, or rooms. The fresco shows the great figures of the classical age and of the Renaissance, all in the same scene.

The most amazing artwork in the Vatican is the painted ceiling of the Sistine Chapel. Michelangelo begins to paint the ceiling in 1508.

In this famous fresco (wall painting) from the Sistine Chapel, Michelangelo pictures the Biblical story of God giving life to Adam in the Garden of Eden.

When he accepts the job, he claims that painting is not his thing—sculpture is. But when Michelangelo completes the ceiling four years later, the result is stunning. The painting shows a history of the Creation (the beginning of human life) as told in the Bible.

The Duomo If you visit Florence, don't miss the Duomo. This domed cathedral rises high above the city. If you climb the twisted stone stairway to the top, you can look out over the red tile rooftops of Florence. Inside the dome is a magnificent painted ceiling. Michelangelo says that he could build a dome "bigger, yes, but not more beautiful." The

The rounded dome of the Duomo still rises over modern-day Florence.

Don't Miss

. . . the Baptistery doors. Artist Lorenzo Ghiberti takes twenty-one years to complete the North Doors and works on the East Doors from 1424 to 1452. The bronze doors feature detailed scenes from the Bible. Because of their beauty, the artist Michelangelo calls the doors the "Gates of Paradise."

Baptistery is part of the Duomo. Built sometime in the A.D. 300s, the Baptistery is one of Florence's oldest buildings. Between 1403 and 1424, sculptor Lorenzo Ghiberti creates amazing bronze doors for the ancient structure.

School You'll find that Renaissance Europeans are hungry for knowledge. Guilds accept only apprentices who can read and write. By the mid-1500s, you will find that half the people of London can read and write. Even the most faraway villages boast at least one local who can read.

In the past, schools taught boys how to be successful merchants and nothing more. But during the Renaissance, teachers add literature, history, and philosophy. Some teachers use texts from classical Greece and Rome. The teachers train students to be educated, intelligent citizens—with good manners, too! If you

48

plan to visit a school, go to Vittorino da Feltre's school in Mantua, Italy. He uses games to teach math and stories to teach literature. Another good school, run by Guarino da Verona, is in Ferrara, Italy. Parents across Italy try to get their kids into these schools. Many boys from wealthy families have private tutors, who may also teach upper-class girls. Unless girls plan to be nuns, few middle-class or poor girls learn to read and write. Instead, most girls learn the important practical skills that they'll need to run a household. Mothers teach their daughters how to clean, sew, and spin.

Some boys go on to study at universities. Students at universities attend lectures and teacher readings. Some universities offer special training in law, medicine, or rhetoric (speaking and writing skills). But many provide students with an education in grammar, arithmetic, logic, music, astronomy, and rhetoric.

VISIT AN ARTIST'S STUDIO

If you want a real treat, visit an artist's studio. Locals gather to watch artists at work. You'll notice that some artists have teams of assistants, who fill in parts of paintings. A master artist might just do the face and hands in a portrait, leaving his assistants to paint the person's clothes. The spectators write down their opinions on the quality of the artist's efforts.

Try to drop in on Leonardo da Vinci while he paints the *Mona Lisa* between 1503 and 1506. This portrait of Lisa del Giocondo will be famous for centuries. Modern-day admirers of the *Mona Lisa* wonder about her smile, which seems mocking, romantic, or just secretive. But you'll be able to ask Lisa del Giocondo exactly what her mysterious expression means!

The Mona Lisa

If you get a chance, peek at da Vinci's notebooks. His detailed, beautiful sketches of faces and machines will amaze you. But you'll find it impossible to read his neat handwriting, even if you know Italian, unless you hold it up to a mirror—he writes backward.

FESTIVALS

No matter when you visit, you're likely to stumble onto a festival—these folks like a party. Religious festivals are held year-round. A few really good festivals are St. John's Eve (June 23), St. Bartholomew's Day (August 24), and the Carnival period before Lent (a period of fasting before Easter). You'll find food, drinks, plays, floats, and even fireworks. People sing and dance around bonfires. The whole town shows up. The last days of Carnival are particularly fun. Women dress as men. Men dress as women. And masters serve their servants.

THEATER

Throughout the Renaissance, groups perform comedy sketches and religious plays. You may see a short play at the end of a dance festival. The plays take place in a castle's courtyard, such as the d'Este family's palace in Ferrara, Italy, in 1486. There, dance festivals end with five or six staged productions.

In the late 1400s, you'll find city-wide religious productions, called *sacre rappresentazioni* in Italian. These representations of characters or subjects from the Bible are especially popular in French cities. Everyone in the city takes part. Powerful religious speakers, known as Preachers of Repentance, call on their audience

The Globe Theater in London is a good place to see Renaissance-era stage stars.

50

Back TO THE FUTURE

The Globe, a theater in London, opens in 1599. It becomes famous as a place to see Shakespeare's plays. Although the theater burned down in the 1600s, archaeologists discovered the foundations of the original Globe Theater in 1989. A modern-day reconstruction of the Globe opened in the 1990s. Builders used the materials and technology that the original, Renaissance builders used.

to turn away from sinful behavior. Some events fill the city square and send people up on the roofs for a better view. Some result in problems with crowd control and damage. After the sermon, you may spot a "bonfire of vanities." Locals burn books, paintings, wigs, and other objects that they think are vain and sinful.

Later in the Renaissance, secular theater really takes off. Writers create plays that are performed in royal courts and in the homes of aristocrats. Rich patrons pay for theater companies that ordinary people flock to see. By the end of the 1500s in England, Shakespeare's plays are wildly popular.

WHERE TO FIND SPORTS & RECREATION

Children play games in the village square.

GAMES

Chess is a favorite board game during the Renaissance. Renaissance Europeans think it's fun to play. They also see their society mirrored in the game. After all, kings, queens, bishops, knights, and castles are parts of everyday Renaissance life. The upper classes enjoy the game, as do ordinary people, who play in local taverns.

SPORTS

If you're a sports fan, you'll have plenty to see in Renaissance Europe. Locals cheer at horse races. And they like races featuring donkeys, cattle, and pigs. The races take place right on the city streets. You may be able to watch from the upstairs window of an inn.

Check out tournaments and jousts, but be prepared for violence. Men on horseback carry lances (long spears). The horses charge forward, and the rider attempts to spear a ring with the point of his lance. In another game, the rider tries to knock away a spinning board. If the rider isn't careful, the board can smack into him painfully.

Some tournaments feature vicious fake battles between groups of armed knights. Locals know that the games are practice for real wars. You may also see mock fights in city squares.

Many other Renaissance sports are violent, too. Adults cheer bulls, bears, or other animals being teased, tortured, injured, and even killed. Torturing and executing criminals is also a spectator sport here. People cheer and boo as the prisoners say their final words to the crowd.

CHECK OUT THE PAINTINGS

In modern times, Renaissance art is in museums all over the world. But during the Renaissance, you won't find any museums. Most paintings decorate the homes of rich and powerful patrons, who ask the artists to create certain pieces of art. The patrons pay for supplies and living expenses while the artist works. Patrons donate some of the art to

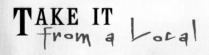

TAKE IT from a Local

[I saw a] completely perfect [portrait of a certain] woman of Florence, done in the size of life.

—the cardinal of Aragon, visiting the home of Leonardo da Vinci in 1517, spotting the Mona Lisa among da Vinci's other paintings

Some Renaissance painters choose everyday scenes for their lifelike portraits. But even though the theme of this picture is casual, the girls are wearing their finest clothes.

churches and monasteries, which also support artists. Visit the refectory (dining hall) of the Dominican monastery of Santa Maria delle Grazie in Milan. There, you'll be able to see Leonardo da Vinci's famous *The Last Supper*. A local in 1517 says that the painting is "wonderfully excellent although it is beginning to spoil." There's a complainer in every crowd.

Renaissance painters experiment with new techniques to make their creations look very realistic. The artists use careful shading to make figures appear three-dimensional. Mathematics helps calculate angles. The artists paint faraway objects small and close-up objects big, as they seem in real life. The painters experiment with ways of arranging objects and with what subjects they paint. Renaissance-era art historian Giorgio Vasari says that by the time Michelangelo dies in 1564, "the three fine arts [painting, sculpture, and architecture] have been brought to a state of absolute perfection."

Cabinets of Curiosities

In the late 1400s and the 1500s, wealthy lawyers, physicians, and nobles create "cabinets of curiosities." The collections include unusual, weird, rare, or beautiful objects. Many collectors choose items from nature, such as mysterious (in the Renaissance) fossils, sparkling crystals, or valuable gems. You may see a stuffed armadillo from the New World (the Americas) or a mummified cat. Some cabinets have stuffed pelicans, crocodiles, a huge elephant, or even a fierce rhino. Illustrated books might be mingled with this stuff.

Some collections fill good-sized closets, but others stuff large rooms. In Florence, Piero de Medici's cabinet of curiosities has a red, white, and green ceiling decorated with twelve round pottery tiles. Each tile is painted with a scene from a different month of the year.

WHERE TO STAY

PRIVATE HOMES

Out in the countryside, inns can be few and far between, so you'll probably spend at least one night in a stranger's home. Don't worry. Many people welcome guests who can share a little news from far-off places. The home of a well-off peasant may be your only choice. The towering pile in front of the house is the dung heap. Don't expect comfort inside

Renaissance homes are crowded, noisy, and dirty. People eat, cook, and keep livestock in one large room.

the large house, which will be made of wood, mud, and thatch. Once you're inside, you'll see that the house is big because it's the barn, too. Pigs, chickens, and even cattle share the cold, dark, smelly space. The storage areas for corn, straw, and hay are also inside the house.

The family lives in a single room. When bedtime comes, mom, pop, the grandparents, and the kids crawl into one big bed. Even a few

Almost all the floors are of clay and rushes from
the marshes, so carelessly renewed that the
foundation sometimes remains for twenty years,
harboring, there below, spittle and vomit and
wine of dogs and men, beer... remnants of
fishes, and other filth unnameable.
—*Desiderius Erasmus, describing typical
Renaissance peasant homes*

chickens or pigs pile on. And of course, the straw mattresses crawl with
bedbugs, lice, and other vermin. Don't expect that, as a guest, you'll get
a room to yourself. You won't even get your own bed! Good manners
require a host to invite a visitor to make one more in the family bed.
Good manners mean that you'll accept the kind offer. Really poor peasants live in shacks with roofs that let in rain and wind. They'll have a
log for a pillow and no bed at all.

Although you'll be able to find an inn in cities, you may prefer to stay
in someone's home. If you stay with someone wealthy, wooden beams
will hold up the ceilings. Tiles, and perhaps a carpet, may cover the
floor. Tapestries cover the walls. The windows will have tiny, thick panes
of glass held together with lead. You'll find a "draw-to chamber" for private meetings and a "parler" for meals and larger gatherings.

A prosperous merchant's house may be two or even three stories high.
On the ground floor, the merchant works in a shop with large shutters
that open to the street. On the first floor, a large kitchen serves as a
dining room. In a big fireplace, a huge fire burns for cooking, light, and
heat. A table and uncomfortable chairs sit in another part of the kitchen.

If you open one of the big chests that appear in most rooms, you'll
find clothes, linens, or even dishes. Many of the chests are works of art.
Brides' chests, for example, have rich carvings or lovely paintings deco-
rating the sides. You may spot jugs, vases, mirrors, or books that show a
family's wealth. Upstairs you'll probably find a bedroom with a huge
four-poster bed. Many beds are so big that they have to be built inside

the rooms (they wouldn't fit through the door). Servants sleep in trundle beds that pull out from under the big bed.

If you are lucky enough to stay with someone who is really rich, you may be in for quite a treat. Rich Florentines build *palazzi*, or townhouses, that reflect classical influences. Columns and arches help support elegant structures. Many have central courtyards, an important part of homes in ancient Greece and Rome.

Jacques Duché's Paris mansion, built in the 1400s, is awesome. Costly furs fill some rooms. Others contain musical instruments, crossbows, or suits of armor. Some have carpets woven with gold thread—not just gold-colored, but real gold! A visitor once said of the home's luxury, "There is a study where the walls are covered in precious stones and spices which give out a delicious odor."

Unlike common folk, wealthy people have several rooms in their houses. These people enjoy a meal and a fire in their dining room.

PUBLIC ACCOMMODATIONS

Inns dot the main roadways across the countryside. You'll also find inns clustered outside the city gates and in certain parts of the cities themselves. If you don't plan to stay with a local in a city, the guards at the gate may issue you a pass to an inn. The innkeeper will sign the pass, which you will be expected to present to the guards when you leave.

If you stay at a monastery, you may meet other travelers.

Don't plan on arriving in a city late at night. Innkeepers frown on it. Honest people aren't usually outdoors after dark. In addition, as the locals say, "He who comes late has a poor supper and a worse bed."

In some areas, competition is so tough that inn workers may meet you on the road and offer to carry your bags to their inn. In other places, you'll really have to keep your eyes peeled to find an inn. A good tip is to look for a colorful sign. Many inns have names such as "The Lion," "The Red Cap," or "The Bell." So the sign may be painted with a picture of a lion, a red cap, or a bell. A really tiny inn may have just a leafy branch or piece of grapevine hung over the door.

In Spain, inns called *ventas* are like farmhouses. Guests sleep in their clothes on large benches. In a German inn, visitors may crowd into a single feather bed. In France, travelers get a bed for their servant. Guests hang out in the dining room. They gather to talk about their travels. Some Renaissance inns have fiddlers or other entertainers.

Some inns are nice, but many are dirty. And you're as likely to be robbed inside an inn as you are on the road. Innkeepers have even been known to set up robberies and murders.

You can also stay at a countryside monastery (a place where monks live). The clergy there offer free shelter and a meal to all travelers. However, if you have money, you are expected to make a donation.

WHAT TO EAT

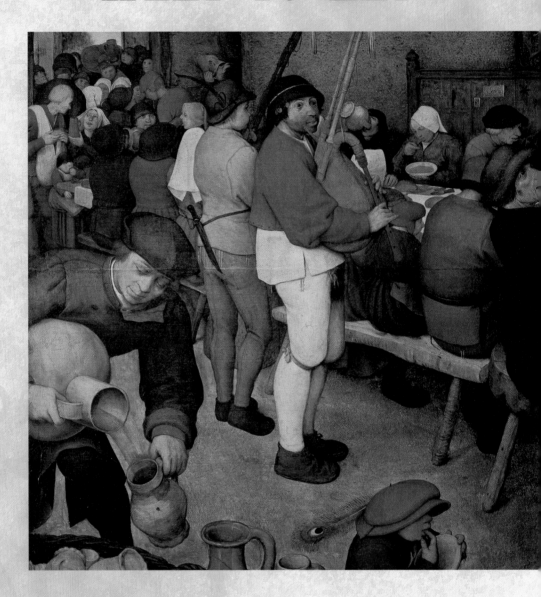

MEALTIME

There are only two meals a day in Renaissance Europe—breakfast between 9:00 and 10:00 in the morning, and supper at 5:00 in the evening. If you can, eat with a local family. Otherwise, visit an inn. Strangers share tables and even trenchers, long wooden boards or slabs of bread shared by several people. Use your hands (that's right!) to take food from a serving plate on the table. Put it on the part of the trencher

There's plenty to eat and drink at this peasant's wedding feast.

in front of you. Don't worry, others will do the same. You'll get a knife, but forks are rare. The ones you see will have only two long tines. Some travelers bring their own silverware.

If you find you are hungry while walking around a major city, you can usually find places to buy food in the market area. If it's a market day, you'll find stalls selling tasty snacks, such as meat pies.

A Splendid Feast

There's a world of difference between the diet of a peasant and the diet of a wealthy noble. Rich folks dine on fifteen to twenty dishes at an everyday dinner. The rich try to outdo each other with lavish feasts featuring dazzling dishes heavily flavored with expensive spices. Some hosts even sprinkle gold dust on the food. Eaters believe that the gold dust is good for the heart. Banquets become so expensive that laws are passed to try to limit them. But the feasts continue anyway.

Dining on a Budget

The main foods in Renaissance Europe are soups, mushes (grain cooked with water), and breads. Wheat, rye, barley, oats, and other grains are big here. The most common meal is a bowl of thin soup made from an ingredient such as watercress, cabbage, dried peas, fish, or cheese. Basically, cooks make soups from leftover scraps or whatever

A fruit seller offers grapes, peaches, melons, berries, and other sweet treats.

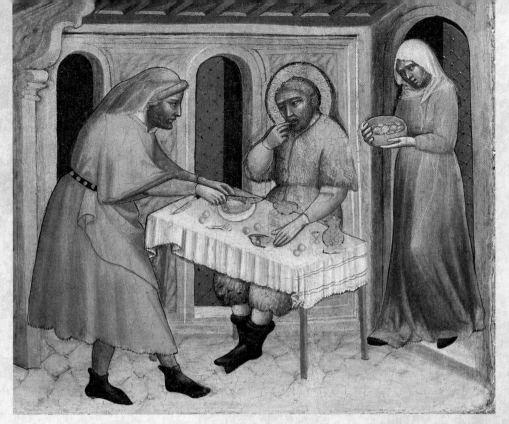

If you really need a meal, stop in at a monastery. They'll feed you free of charge.

they happen to have plenty of. Add a chunk of black bread, and that's what people eat most of the time. Milk, butter, and hard cheese are expensive. Fish is available only near coasts and rivers. Except for salted (preserved) fish, seafood isn't a big part of many people's diets. People do eat eggs and poultry, especially in the countryside.

FOOD TO TRY

- *Zafferano*—colored jellies made in Florence from almond-milk and shaped like men or animals

- Oxen salted to prevent spoiling, then boiled in a large copper vat

- Stag roasted in the fireplace until crispy, cut into quarters, and covered with a steaming pepper sauce

Many peasants raise extra poultry and sell the birds on market days.

WHERE'S THE BEEF?

If you dine with peasants, you won't get much meat. Most families are lucky to have meat once a month, for a couple of reasons. It costs a lot to feed animals. And when an animal is butchered, it must be salted to preserve the meat (there are no refrigerators here). Salt can be pricey. Peasants who have pigs will generally sell them in town or to the local manor (house of a lord) rather than eat them.

FOODS TO TRY, at your own risk

- *Fegatelli*—a sausage made from liver
- Black pudding (made from the blood of a pig)

Now Hear This

To make Sauce Aliper for rostid beef tak broun bred and stepe it in venygar and toiste it and streyne it and stampe garlik and put ther to pouder of pepper and salt and boile it a litill and serue it. [To make aliper sauce for roast beef, soak brown bread in vinegar; strain it; add pressed garlic, ground pepper, and salt; boil a little; and serve.]

—recipe for Sauce Aliper from A Noble Boke of Cookry, ca. 1467

Renaissance people—especially rich folks at feasts—eat birds such as herons, swans, peacocks, larks, robins, and storks. Cooks pluck and roast the birds, then put the feathers back in place to make a dramatic presentation.

Locals also eat wild game, such as deer and boar. Seal, porpoise, and whale appear from time to time. People eat goat, hedgehog, and dormice. Actually, they'll eat nearly anything that walks or flies.

WOULD YOU CARE FOR A BEVERAGE WITH THAT?

Water is not popular as a beverage (it's filthy). You will not find coffee or tea, either. Kids drink milk. In Italy and France, grown-ups drink wine with their meals. In England and Germany, beer or ale is the adults' beverage of choice. People drink huge quantities. When Henry VII and Henry VIII are kings of England, the government gives out a gallon of beer a day for every person.

WHERE TO FIND SOUVENIRS

THE MARKET

If you want to buy a souvenir, the market is the first place to look. Some marketplaces are set off from villages and are surrounded by a wall. Guards will make sure you pay a small admission fee (the money might go to the king). Other markets are held in a city square or even in a special marketplace. Most markets occur at certain times, like on a specific saint's day. On that day, the regular shops might close. Just to buy a loaf of bread for breakfast, you'll have to go to the market. But it's not a sight to be missed. Early in the morning, farmers bring goods into town. They sell vegetables, meat, and fish at stalls. Merchants set up booths overflowing with exotic spices, rich fabrics, and other goods. You may even spot barbers shaving people in the open air. Games may be set up. Keep an eye on your purse—pickpockets and other criminals will be hard at work.

WORKSHOPS

In the larger cities, stores sell silks, textiles, gold jewelry, and other items. But some areas specialize in certain products. Since you'll be traveling, you may find it cheaper to buy directly from craftspeople. Here are a few tips. Look for the jewelers' district in Venice, Italy. You can admire outstanding jewelry, gem-studded helmets, elaborate gold pieces, and

Some Renaissance Europeans collect beautiful, interesting, or unusual objects. Jewelry, coins, books, and artwork are some of the things you may want to bring home.

This sixteenth-century French tapestry shows a harvest scene in a vineyard.

jeweled crowns. Genoa, Italy, is definitely the spot to buy the best velvet. In Nuremberg, Germany, you won't want to miss the clocks and locks. Brussels, Belgium, is the place to find amazing tapestries. The weavers use different colors of thread, creating thick fabric woven with detailed pictures. Some tapestries show famous scenes, while others tell well-known stories. These take so much work and skill to make that almost any tapestry costs more than a painting. But keep in mind that a painting won't keep your walls from letting in the cold—a good tapestry will.

PAINTINGS

With so many outstanding artists, a painting can be the perfect Renaissance souvenir. You should expect to pay one hundred or more florins for a painting by a good Florentine artist. Of course, you don't need to be in Florence to find a good painter. Ask around in any trading center of Europe, and you'll probably find several artists from which to choose.

Think about paying an artist to create an original painting of anything you want. In the Renaissance, people commission (pay an artist to make) a portrait of themselves or their families. Most sitters ask that the painting show off their most expensive or impressive possessions, such as splendid clothes and jewelry. Or people might pose with objects that tell others about their interests or their job. You might choose to be painted looking at a map or holding a compass to show your interest in travel.

Back TO THE FUTURE

While you're visiting Renaissance Europe, notice how bright and colorful the famous paintings of the era are. When you see these same paintings in modern-day museums—hundreds of years later—you'll see a big difference. Over the years (as you can see on this painting of a lady with her pet weasel), the

paints fade, the varnish darkens, and dirt clings to the surface. Modern-day art restorers use sophisticated techniques to clean and repair old paintings, but it is impossible to recapture their original brilliance.

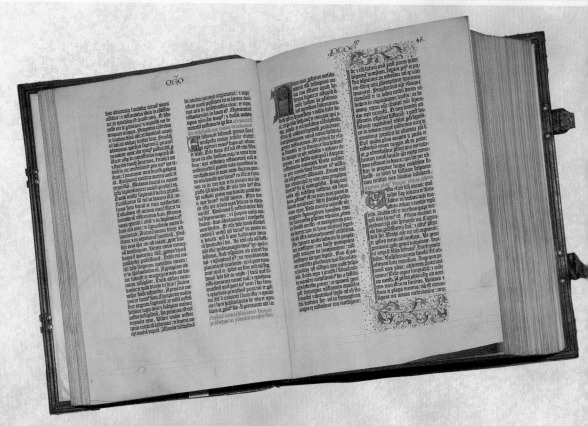

One of the most famous Renaissance-era books is Johannes Gutenberg's Bible. Your trip might provide you the opportunity to buy a copy.

BOOKS

You're probably used to cheap paperback books. But you should know that before the late 1400s, books are very expensive. It's very rare for an ordinary person to own a book. One book costs about as much as a skilled artisan can earn in a month. In the early Renaissance, only churches, universities, kings, and some nobles have collections of books. Even the biggest collections contain fewer than three hundred titles. (Compare that to a modern-day public library in a large city, which may have more than two million books.) In fact, books are so rare and valuable that at least one church chains them to desks. To make books, a team of artists, often monks, slowly copies the text by hand.

Try to get a look at the most famous book of all time. It's the Bible, printed in 1457 and 1458 by Johannes Gensfleisch Gutenberg. (By the way, he prefers to be called Johannes Gutenberg because "Gensfleisch" means "gooseflesh" or "goose bumps.") Gutenberg's mechanical press makes printing large quantities of books possible for the first time. The press, which uses movable type, makes it cheaper to make books. All of a sudden, large numbers of people all across Europe can afford books. Through reading, Europeans come to share the ideas and knowledge of the Renaissance philosophers. Practical, how-to knowledge spreads, too. Textbooks are among the first books printed. For example, a book on mathematics, published in Portugal in 1519, helps merchants better manage their money.

Rich locals pay to print fine books. Printers bind the books in covers made from leather, silver, silk, velvet, or gold. Look for printed books with hand-painted illustrations, often decorated with real gold. If you go book shopping in the 1460s or 1470s, you'll buy books from a printing company. But by the 1480s, you'll find booksellers in most big cities. When you travel in the countryside, you may run into a peddler selling books that he carries in a heavy bag hanging from his neck. If you visit Germany in 1500, you will be able to choose from 25,000 different books.

The famous German artist Albrecht Dürer sees that printed works will reach more people than paintings. He carves pictures into wood blocks, which are inked and then pressed onto paper. The woodcuts are an easy way to get his work out to the public.

Books are a powerful way to spread new ideas. Some of the ideas make the Catholic Church angry. The Church begins to censor (control) what is written in books. Many authors run into problems with the censors. One book, titled *On the Revolutions of the Celestial Spheres*, is by a Polish astronomer named Nicolaus Copernicus. First published in 1543, the book demonstrates that the earth is not the center of our planetary system (as Renaissance thinkers, following the ancient Greeks and Romans, believe it to be). Copernicus's book says that the sun is at the center, and that the planets, including earth, revolve around it. The Church believes that God, according to the Bible, placed the earth at the center of the universe. The Church's censors declare that the book is heretical (anti-religious). The book is banned by the Catholic Church until 1835.

How to Stay
Safe & Healthy

A doctor and a servant tend the needs of a sick person.

Balance Your Humors
& Call Me in the Morning

The locals believe that the body contains four humors: blood, yellow bile, phlegm, and black bile. These spread through the body in veins and arteries. If the balance among the humors is upset, the person becomes ill. The humors also affect personality. Too much black bile causes melancholy (sadness), for example.

One way the locals try to restore the balance among the humors is by removing blood. Some doctors puncture a patient's arm to allow blood to flow out of the body. Others apply leeches, sluglike creatures that suck a person's blood. Leaching is thought to lower body temperature and to calm the patient. But the practice can also lead to infection and make a person weak because of the blood loss.

Many locals believe that kings and queens have healing powers. In the 1500s, nearly 17,500 people kneel before King Francis I of France. He touches each person on the head to cure him or her of scrofula, a swelling of the lymph glands. The disease is known as "the king's evil," because only a king is believed to be able to cure it.

Local Diseases & Dangers

Count yourself lucky—you've already been born. In the Renaissance, that's the most dangerous part of a young person's life. Many babies die at childbirth. Just because you've survived birth doesn't mean you'll be safe. Avoid cuts and scrapes, because even a small break in the skin can get infected. And an infection can be deadly. Renaissance Europeans don't have antibiotics, modern-day medicines that fight infections.

Religious groups run many hospitals. These institutions provide food, shelter, and prayer for pilgrims, the old, the poor, and the sick. One of the oldest hospitals is Santa Maria Nuova in Florence. By the way, if you have a wound, you will have to go to a barber for treatment.

Renaissance doctors experiment with new practices. The most common treatment for gunshot wounds (pouring boiling oil on them) changes when a physician runs out of boiling oil. He uses cold salve instead. His patients heal better with the salve.

Side Trip Trivia If you visit western Africa during this period, you can see the Songhai Empire. There, physicians perform advanced procedures, such as removing cataracts. They also know that mosquitoes spread malaria.

Other doctors follow his lead. Medical books help spread the word
about new treatments.

Many Renaissance Europeans have skin diseases, such as a fungus
called ringworm. A big reason so many people have skin diseases is
because they wear the same clothes day after day without washing
them. Other common complaints include sprains, catarrh (colds), and
cataracts (an eye condition).

Physicians—who study medicine for years—are expensive here.
Without good painkillers, pretty much anything the doctor does is
going to hurt. For operations, amputations, or repairing wounds, four
strong men hold the patient down. Rather than go through the painful
and often unsuccessful procedures, locals rely on herbs and medicinal
plants instead.

DISASTERS, CATASTROPHES, & OTHER ANNOYANCES

Famine Famine strikes about every four years. If you travel during one
of these periods, expect terrible conditions. If you stay with a peasant
family, you'll be able to tell that it's famine time because everyone is
naked. People sell their clothes to buy food. You'll also see people eating
bark, grass, or even clay.

Plague The Black Death (bubonic plague) takes many lives during the
Renaissance. The disease is named for the black swellings that
are one of its symptoms. In 1471, for example, 10 percent of the English
population die during an outbreak of plague.

Citizens bring a plague victim outside of the town. They will carry the sick person to a shrine (a small place of worship) in the countryside, where they hope the person will be miraculously healed.

The locals don't know that the plague is spread by plague-carrying fleas that bite rats, which become infected, too. The fleas bite humans, who then become sick. Physicians debate whether plague is contagious or not. Most people consider it a punishment from God. Some feel it is useless, or even dangerous, to fight the will of God by trying to control the spread of the disease. Others believe that stray dogs spread the illness. Cities order all dogs to be killed. This doesn't work.

The plague affects more poor people than rich. The rats that spread the disease live in the cellars and alleys where the poor live. Fleas thrive where people are too poor to have hot water to bathe and to wash clothing and sheets. During the second half of the 1500s, governments set up ways to deal with the plague. Streets are closed off, ships are kept at port, shops and inns are closed, and public gatherings are forbidden. Victims of the disease (and their families) may be boarded up in their homes.

As a traveler, plan for delays and disappointments. Guards posted outside some of the cities turn travelers away. Or they may keep you in a hospital for forty days to make sure you don't have the plague. Infected people must wear a white armband or carry a white stick to warn others.

77

WATCH FOR WARS

You may have thought that by scheduling your trip between the Hundred Years' War of 1337–1453 (between England and France) and the Thirty Years' War of 1618–1648 (a general European war, fought mainly in Germany), you could avoid the dangers of travel during wartime. But Renaissance Europe is not a peaceful place.

Peasants revolt against landowners. Rulers of countries fight over land and power. No year is free from violent conflicts. When Charles VIII of France invades Italy in 1494, a period of foreign invasions begins. Here are some of the highlights from the next fifty years of warfare:

France invades Italy and conquers Naples in 1495. Spain ousts the French from Naples in 1496. But three years later, France invades Italy again and conquers Milan. In 1502 the French and the Spaniards in Italy go to war. Spain conquers Naples in 1504, but the French defeat the Spanish at Ravenna and the Swiss conquer Milan in 1512. France invades Italy a third time and recaptures Milan in 1515. The Spanish defeat the French in Italy ten years later, but the troops of the Holy Roman Empire sack Rome in 1527. The determined French invade Italy for a fourth time in 1555. The next year, Philip II becomes king of Spain and ruler of Milan, Naples, and Sicily. And in 1559, France finally gets the message and stops invading Italy.

Tech Talk

Newly improved cannons have forced Renaissance Europeans to rebuild and strengthen fortresses and town walls. The cannons can smash and topple the high towers built in earlier times. Using mathematical concepts, engineers design low, star-shaped fortresses. Military engineers mount cannons on bastions, or solid, angled structures level with the fortress walls. Siege warfare has sparked inventions such as a portable cannon that fires a rocketlike missile.

Opposing armies square off in this early Renaissance battle scene.

Renaissance soldiers are healthy men between the ages of fifteen and sixty. Only the clergy, lawyers, heads of households, and household servants aren't forced into the military.

During wartime, large groups of soldiers walk across the countryside from battle to battle. They drag heavy cannons, which chew up and destroy the roads. Passing through a town, an army takes the food, tramples the growing crops in the fields, and takes horses and cattle. Soldiers even cut down the trees for firewood. The roving armies also spread disease. And in some cases, the troops simply burn down the town and murder any residents they find.

You will want to avoid a siege. Walls surround most cities. So an attacking army often settles down outside the city to wait until the people inside get so hungry that they surrender. Of course, the attackers will keep trying to bash down the walls. Depending upon the length of the siege (it can last for months), food and supplies will get scarce.

If you don't help defend the city, you'll be punished or even killed. Townspeople may kick out people, such as children and disabled people, who eat the scarce supply of food but can't help defend the city.

They may be forced outside the town walls to survive on grass and other plants. They may also be captured—or killed—by the enemy.

Women repair breaks in the city's walls. They use picks and shovels to build defenses inside the city. In Siena, Italy, during a siege in 1552–1553, all women between the ages of twelve and fifty are part of the city's army. Soldiers from the attacking army do not distinguish between men with guns and women with shovels. All are considered enemies and may be killed in action.

Defenders who survive a siege may not survive an attacker's victory party. These battles often mark the end of years and years of bitter conflict. When the conquerors finally enter a fallen city, they treat citizens with unimaginable cruelty. The soldiers may torture or kill women and children, leave the wounded to die, and burn down the entire city.

If you can, travel with a group of people who are headed in the same direction you are. Your trip will be safer and more entertaining.

LAW & ORDER

Renaissance Europe is not the place to see what you can get away with. These folks are tough on crime. Real tough. Common punishments include cutting off ears, plucking out eyes, and ripping out tongues.

Even with these harsh punishments, there's still a lot of crime during the Renaissance. You should take care while walking at night in the cities. Watchmen patrol the streets and stretch chains across the entrances of streets to block fleeing robbers. You may still find thieves lurking in dark alleys. If you are going to travel across the countryside, you may want to travel with a group. You can also hire an escort to avoid being a victim of highway robbery, kidnapping, or even murder. Many travelers hide their valuables. Try sewing your coins into the linings of your clothes. One local has success by putting his money in the bottom of a box and covering it with "a stinking ointment for scabs." The robbers throw the box down, leaving the money behind.

IMPORTANT

Safety Tip

People accused of crimes in England really benefit from their education. They can plead "benefit of clergy." If they are able to sign their own names and read a couple of lines from the Bible, they get lighter sentences. When two burglars who are caught breaking into the home of the Earl of Sussex in 1613 take this test, one flunks and is hanged. The other passes and gets off easy. He is only branded (scarred by burning) on the thumb.

The Catholic Church has its own courts and gives out its own punishments. These generally involve some form of humiliation. A person might have to wear a sackcloth (a roughly woven, baggy outfit) with no pants and bare feet. Another punishment is to be banned from church or shunned (rejected) by other people. Severe measures involve forced fasts (going without food), taking the offender's money (all of it), whipping, or clubbing.

If you travel to Japan during this period, don't offend one of the samurai (warriors) who serve local lords. The samurai are allowed to sever the head of anyone who provokes them on a point of honor, as long as they notify the authorities afterward.

A religious court may sentence serious criminals to walk a long distance barefoot. Long distance isn't just from home into town. It's from Paris to, say, Rome or Jerusalem—distances of hundreds or even thousands of miles. To add to the pain, the offender may have to wear chains around the neck and wrists or leg irons around the ankles.

In Geneva religious reformer John Calvin leads a very strict society. For example, people must name their children after figures from the Bible's Old Testament. One man, who insisted on calling his newborn son Claude, was imprisoned for four days. Even the wrong hairstyle can land you in jail. Failing to attend church regularly can result in being burned at the stake. And unmarried women who become pregnant are drowned.

WHO'S WHO IN RENAISSANCE EUROPE

CATHERINE DE MÉDICIS

If you visit Italy in 1530, you may meet a remarkable eleven-year-old girl named Catherine. As a member of the important and powerful Medici family, Catherine is taken hostage in a battle between her family and the city of Florence. The Florentine authorities threaten to put Catherine on the wall of the city while her own family's soldiers attack. She convinces the authorities that she wants to be a nun, so the Florentines change their minds.

By 1530 the Medici troops have won. Catherine has become a famous hero, but she doesn't become a nun. At the age of fourteen, she marries another fourteen-year-old—Henry, the son of the king of France. In 1547 Henry inherits the throne and Catherine becomes queen.

TAKE IT from a Local

I hope it will be recognized that women are more inclined to conserve the kingdom than those who have put it in the condition in which it is.

—*Catherine de Médicis*

If you visit in the 1550s, you will see that Catherine has become a strong, active partner to the king. Nevertheless, when her husband dies, the law prevents her from inheriting the crown because she is a woman. Three of her sons will become kings of France, one will become king of Poland, and a daughter will be queen of Navarre (an area of Spain and France).

CHRISTINE DE PISAN

In the early Renaissance, you may hear about the French poet and writer Christine de Pisan. She is born in Venice, but she grows up at the court of King Charles V of France. Her father is the king's astrologer. Her husband dies when she is only in her twenties, so she begins writing books to help support her three children. She writes love poems, verses mourning her husband, and even a biography of King Charles V. But she is best known for her book *The Book of the City of Ladies* (1405), which is a history of good and courageous women.

ERASMUS

Desiderius Erasmus, from Rotterdam in the Netherlands, is the greatest humanist scholar in northern Europe. His book *Praise of Folly* criticizes superstition and ignorance. *Adagia*, a collection of sayings from ancient Greek and Roman authors, contains his moral and philosophical beliefs. He disputes with Martin Luther and edits the Bible's New Testament in Greek. Erasmus's letters to other scholars and his popular writings help spread humanist ideas across Europe. He visits the court of England's King Henry VIII and influences the thinking of other powerful European leaders.

LEONARDO DA VINCI

Leonardo da Vinci is the ultimate "Renaissance Man." (This expression has come to mean someone who is educated and skillful in many areas.) He's so brilliant that he becomes an expert in biology, engineering, language, music, philosophy, architecture, art, and many other fields. Leonardo da Vinci has hundreds of ideas, some of which won't become realities for hundreds of years. He sketches guided missiles, submarines, flying machines, and parachutes. Some of his ideas are built in his lifetime. He designs a canal system with locks, which allow boats to move safely between waters of different heights. His system is still used in modern times. And he's a painter, too. (Remember the *Mona Lisa?*)

MARTIN LUTHER

You may hear a lot about a German named Martin Luther. He is a Catholic priest who objects to many of the Church's practices. His ideas for reforming the Church will become the foundation for a new branch of Christianity—Protestantism. (One Protestant faith, Lutheranism, will be named for him.) If you want to see him in action, go to the church at Wittenberg, Germany, on October 31, 1517. In the Renaissance, church doors are kind of like public bulletin boards. Luther nails up a list of ninety-five objections he has to the Church's practices.

Martin Luther goes too far when he threatens that, unless things change, true Christians will settle matters with the sword. The Church excommunicates Luther in June 1520 and forbids Christians from listening to him or even looking at him. In response, Luther burns the bull (the official letter from the Pope) that carries the orders. In 1521 the Church outlaws him from all territories of the Holy Roman Empire.

FERDINAND MAGELLAN

When you first meet Spaniard Ferdinand Magellan, you may not be impressed. He's short, has rough skin and a bushy black beard, and walks with a limp. He doesn't look like the greatest explorer of the 1500s. But the people who know him see that he's a careful, tough, ambitious, imaginative dreamer who refuses to accept defeat.

A good time to catch him is in the beginning of September 1519 at Sanlúcar de Barrameda, Spain. He is preparing a fleet of five ships, which he intends to take around the world on a two-year voyage (it will actually take three). He checks every detail, personally testing each board, inspecting every rope, and supervising the loading of food and other supplies. For the 265 crew members, he's ordered great quantities of rice, beans, flour, onions, raisins, and other foods. Let's hope they like pickled pork (he's packing nearly three tons of it) and anchovies (two hundred barrels)! The ships set sail on September 19, 1519. He dies before the journey ends, but his crew circumnavigates (circles) the globe. It's an amazing feat. The trip makes Europeans see that Europe is only a small part of a big world.

PARACELSUS

Philip Aureolus Theophrastus Bombast von Hohenheim (see, isn't Paracelsus easier?) is a rebel with a cause. He hopes to improve medical care for patients. You may find him somewhat of a braggart—for instance, he gives himself the name Paracelsus, which means "greater than Celsus," a famous Roman encyclopedist.

But he is way ahead of his time. After studying medicine, he decides that most Renaissance doctors don't seem to help patients at all. In fact, many seem to make the patients worse. He spends ten years traveling throughout Europe and to Russia, Turkey, and the Middle East. He talks to local experts about medicine and healing.

Paracelsus is a pioneer. He is the first person to notice that certain jobs, such as mining, put workers at risk for certain illnesses. Paracelsus also experiments with chemicals. He develops powerful drugs to fight diseases—linking chemistry and medicine forever. He stands behind the idea that patients' health can be improved through diet, environment, and even the behavior of the people around them.

Now Hear This

The best of our popular physicians are the ones who do the least harm. But unfortunately some poison their patients with mercury, and others purge or bleed them to death . . . there are others who care a great deal more for their own profit than for the health of their patients.

—*Paracelsus*

PREPARING FOR THE TRIP

CREATE A PAPER MUSEUM!

Many Renaissance Europeans had no room for a cabinet of curiosities. Instead, they kept "paper museums"—books filled with notes and drawings of interesting things they'd seen and done. In the spirit of the Renaissance, make a little book and then use it to hold your own paper museum.

> four sheets of 8½-by-11-inch paper
> a hole punch
> an 8-inch-long ribbon or string

Take the four sheets of paper and fold them in half. Punch two holes on the fold. Loop a string or ribbon from one hole to the other and then tie it in a tight knot. This will bind your book together. (If you run out of space on your pages, you can untie the knot and slip more paper into the booklet.)

Organize your paper museum by "exhibit." Use a page for each exhibit. You could list interesting objects that you've seen in museums and out in the world. You could choose boats, statues, horses, toys, fossils, and places.

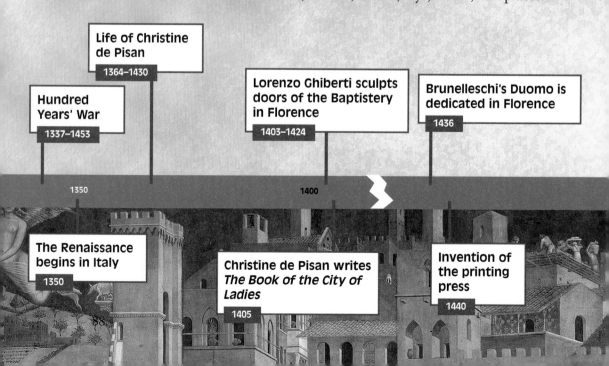

Life of Christine de Pisan
1364–1430

Hundred Years' War
1337–1453

Lorenzo Ghiberti sculpts doors of the Baptistery in Florence
1403–1424

Brunelleschi's Duomo is dedicated in Florence
1436

1350

1400

The Renaissance begins in Italy
1350

Christine de Pisan writes *The Book of the City of Ladies*
1405

Invention of the printing press
1440

Be creative! Tell where you saw it and when you saw it. Then describe it in detail. You could even draw a little picture of the object or place!

PAINT A PORTRAIT

In the Renaissance, many people chose to have their portraits painted. Try painting portraits of friend or family members! You will need:

> paints, watercolors, colored pencils, or crayons
> paintbrushes
> thick paper to paint on
> a person to paint

Pose your subject (the person you will paint). Try to pick a comfortable position for him or her to stand or sit in. As Renaissance painters did, you can choose to paint your subject with objects that show what he or she likes to do, what his or her job is, or in a setting that shows something else about him or her. If your subjects recently took a tropical vacation, you could paint a tropical background. Or if your subject wants to be an astronaut, you might want to ask your subject to hold a model of a space shuttle. If someone has a really great outfit, that's what he or she should wear. Have fun!

Painting a portrait isn't easy. You might first want to sketch the person in pencil and then use the paints to color your sketch.

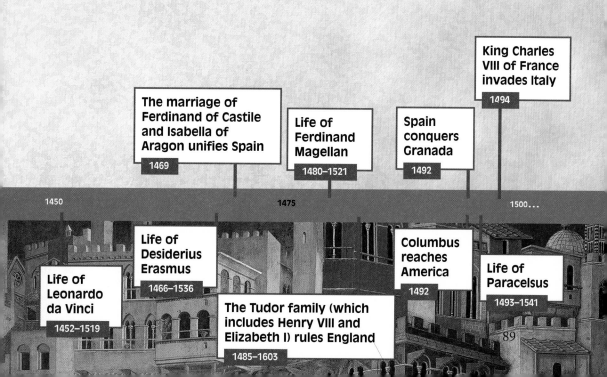

King Charles VIII of France invades Italy
1494

The marriage of Ferdinand of Castile and Isabella of Aragon unifies Spain
1469

Life of Ferdinand Magellan
1480–1521

Spain conquers Granada
1492

1450   1475   1500...

Life of Desiderius Erasmus
1466–1536

Columbus reaches America
1492

Life of Paracelsus
1493–1541

Life of Leonardo da Vinci
1452–1519

The Tudor family (which includes Henry VIII and Elizabeth I) rules England
1485–1603

89

GLOSSARY

apprentice: a person who learns a craft or a trade by working for and studying with someone already skilled in the field

bubonic plague: also known as the Black Death. This fatal bacterial disease kills many Europeans between 1300 and 1600.

city-state: a self-governed community, such as those in Renaissance Italy, that consists of one city and the land surrounding it

duty: a fee charged for transporting goods or for using roads, bridges, waterways, or other transport routes

excommunicate: to banish a person from the Catholic Church, usually as punishment for committing a crime or an action against Church rules

feudalism: a system of government common in Europe from the 800s to the 1500s. Under feudalism, landowners (known as "lords") had power over renters (known as "serfs" or "peasants"), who worked or lived on the land.

humanism: a cultural movement that emerged during the Renaissance. Humanism centered on the importance and dignity of individuals. Humanists were also very interested in the study of literature, history, and philosophy.

pilgrim: a person who travels for religious reasons

printing press: a machine that uses movable type to make printed copies. Movable type can be easily rearranged. In about 1440, Johannes Gutenberg builds a printing press that he uses to produce a famous copy of the Bible.

serf: a member of the non-landowning class in the feudal system. Serfs rent land that they farm to support themselves and their family. Some serfs are legally tied to (forbidden to leave) the land and forbidden to take a different kind of job.

Vatican: a complex of buildings in Rome. The Vatican serves as the headquarters of the Roman Catholic Church and the home of the Pope. The construction of St. Peter's Basilica begins at the Vatican during the Renaissance.

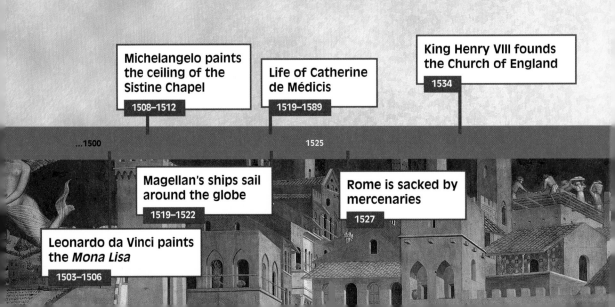

Michelangelo paints the ceiling of the Sistine Chapel
1508–1512

Life of Catherine de Médicis
1519–1589

King Henry VIII founds the Church of England
1534

...1500

1525

Magellan's ships sail around the globe
1519–1522

Rome is sacked by mercenaries
1527

Leonardo da Vinci paints the *Mona Lisa*
1503–1506

Pronunciation Guide

Catherine de Médicis	KAHTH-rihn duh MEHD-ih-chee
Christine de Pisan	krihs-TEEN duh pee-ZAHN
Copernicus	koh-PEHR-nih-kuhs
da Gama, Vasco	dah GAH-muh, VAH-skoh
donjon	DAHN-juhn
ducat	DUH-kuht
Duomo	DWOH-moh
Erasmus, Desiderius	ih-RAZ-muhs, dehs-ih-DEHR-ee-uhs
Ferrara	fuh-RAH-ruh
Gutenberg, Johannes	GOOT-uhn-buhrg, yoh-HAHN-uhs
Leonardo da Vinci	lay-uh-NAHR-doh dah VIHN-chee

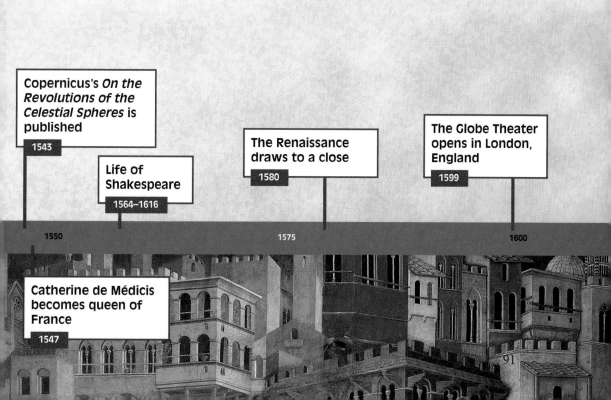

Copernicus's *On the Revolutions of the Celestial Spheres* is published

1543

Life of Shakespeare

1564–1616

The Renaissance draws to a close

1580

The Globe Theater opens in London, England

1599

1550

1575

1600

Catherine de Médicis becomes queen of France

1547

FURTHER READING

Books

Caselli, Giovanni. *The Renaissance and the New World*. New York: Peter Bedrick Books, 1998.

France in Pictures. Minneapolis: Lerner Publications Company, 1998.

Harnett, Cynthia. *The Great House*. Minneapolis: Lerner Publications Company, 1984.

Harnett, Cynthia. *The Writing on the Hearth*. Minneapolis: Lerner Publications Company, 1984.

Howarth, Sarah. *Renaissance People*. Brookfield, CT: Millbrook Press, 1992.

Howarth, Sarah. *Renaissance Places*. Brookfield, CT: Millbrook Press, 1992.

Italy in Pictures. Minneapolis: Lerner Publications Company, 1997.

MacDonald, Fiona. *The World in the Time of Leonardo da Vinci*. Parsippany, NJ: Dillon Press, 1998.

Osman, Karen. *The Italian Renaissance*. San Diego: Lucent Books, 1996.

Pelta, Kathy. *Discovering Christopher Columbus*. Minneapolis: Lerner Publications Company, 1991.

Spence, David, and Tessa Krailing. *Michelangelo and the Renaissance*. Hauppauge, NY: Barron's Educational Series, 1997.

Ventura, Piero. *1492: The Year of the New World*. New York: G. P. Putnam's Sons, 1991.

Wood, Tim. *The Renaissance*. New York: Viking Press, 1993.

Internet Sites

Annenburg/CPB Exhibits. *Explore the Renaissance*. 1998.
<http://www.learner.org/exhibits/renaissance/>

Marszalek, Chris, Linda Mazanek, and Bonnie Panagakis. *Virtual Renaissance*. 1997.
<http://www.twingroves.district96.k12.il.us/Renaissance/guildhall/present.html>

BIBLIOGRAPHY

Camusso, Lorenzo. *Travel Guide to Europe, 1492: Ten Itineraries in the Old World.* New York: Henry Holt and Company, 1990.

Duin, Nancy. *A History of Medicine: From Pre-History to the Year 2000.* New York: Simon & Schuster, 1992.

Hale, J. R. *The Civilization of Europe in the Renaissance.* New York: Atheneum, 1994.

Hale, John R., and the editors of Time-Life Books. *Renaissance.* New York: Time, Inc., 1965.

Hale, J. R. *War and Society in Renaissance Europe, 1450–1620.* New York: St. Martin's Press, 1985.

Jardine, Lisa. *Worldly Goods: A New History of the Renaissance.* New York: Nan A. Talese, 1996.

Manchester, William. *A World Lit Only by Fire: The Medieval Mind and the Renaissance: Portrait of an Age.* Boston: Little, Brown and Company, 1992.

Rabb, Theodore K. *Renaissance Lives: Portraits of an Age.* New York: Pantheon Books, 1993.

Wolfe, Linda. *The Literary Gourmet: Menus from Masterpieces.* New York: Harmony Books, 1985.

INDEX

ABOUT THE AUTHOR

Nancy Day is the author of nine books and forty-five articles for young people. She loves to read and is fascinated with the idea of time travel, which she says is "actually history in a great disguise." Her interest in time travel inspired the Passport to History series. Nancy Day lives with her husband, son, and two cats in a house that was built in 1827—before the Civil War. She often imagines what it would be like to go back in time to meet the shipbuilder who once lived there.

Acknowledgments for Quoted Material pp. 8, 30, 39, as quoted by J. R. Hale, *The Civilization of Europe in the Renaissance* (New York: Atheneum, 1994); p. 43, as quoted by John R. Hale and the editors of Time-Life Books, *Renaissance* (New York: Time, Inc., 1965); p. 53, as quoted by Lorenzo Camusso, *Travel Guide to Europe, 1492: Ten Itineraries in the Old World* (New York: Henry Holt and Company, 1990); p. 58, as quoted by William Manchester, *A World Lit Only by Fire: The Medieval Mind and the Renaissance: Portrait of an Age* (Boston: Little, Brown and Company, 1992); p. 67, as quoted by Linda Wolfe, *The Literary Gourmet: Menus from Masterpieces* (New York: Harmony Books, 1985); p. 83, as quoted by Theodore K. Rabb, *Renaissance Lives: Portraits of an Age* (New York: Pantheon Books, 1993); p. 87, as quoted by Nancy Duin, *A History of Medicine: From Pre-History to the Year 2000* (New York: Simon & Schuster, 1992).

Photo Acknowledgments
The images in this book are used with the permission of: Corbis: (© Archivo Iconografico, S.A) pp. 2, 24 (bottom), 25 (both), 56–57, 86 (bottom), (© Chris Hellier) p. 20, (© Ted Spiegel) p. 24 (top), (© Bettmann) p. 83 (top); Art Resource, NY: (Scala) pp. 6–7, 10, 16–17, 19, 22, 26–27, 28–29, 33, 36, 41, 42, 43, 44, 46–47, 48, 49, 60, 64, 65, 74, 77, 80, 86 (top), (Erich Lessing) pp. 12, 30, 34, 38, 52, 54, 62–63, 66, 71, 84 (bottom), (Victoria & Albert Museum, London) pp. 14, 37, (Art Resource) p. 50, (The Pierpont Morgan Library) pp. 59, 72, (Nimatallah) p. 68, (Giraudon) pp. 70, 84 (top); Bibliothèque Nationale, Paris/The Art Archive, p. 79; British Library, London/Bridgeman Art Library, London/ New York, p. 84 (top); The Granger Collection, p. 85.

Front cover images: Art Resource, NY: (Scala) (upper left), (Vanni) (lower right).